Discovering Jesus

A Discipleship Manual

Spirit Life Ministries International

"...a foundation for many godly generations..."

Spirit Life Ministries International

Discovering Jesus – A Discipleship Manual

Copyright © 2001 by F. Dean Hakcett, Ph.D.

This title is also available as an ebook. Visit www.fdeanhackett.com/store

Requests for information should be addressed to Spirit Life Ministries Publications, Hermiston, Oregon 97838

ISBN: 978-1539930242

All rights reserved. No portion of this publication may be reproduced in a retrieval system, or transmitted in any form or by any means – electronic, mechanical, photocopy, recording, or otherwise – without the express prior permission of Spirit Life Ministries Publications, with the exception of brief excerpts in magazine articles and/or other reviews.

Front Cover design: Stephanie Eidson
Back Cover design: Aaron Hackett
Cover photography: Pixabay
Interior Design: Rosilind Jukić

Printed in the United States of America

I gratefully dedicate this work to my
"Spiritual Father"
Reverend Edward L. Murphy.
He is a man of impeccable integrity and
Christ-like example,
who patiently and lovingly discipled me and
"equipped me for the work of the ministry"

Table of Contents

Introduction 7

Experiencing New Life - Student 9

Experiencing New Life – Student Handout 13

Discovering the Mark of the Family Covenant 19

Discovering the Mark of the Family Covenant – Student Handout 23

Discovering the Family Dynamic 27

Discovering the Family Dynamic – Student Handout 29

The Beauty of Spiritual Language 33

The Beauty of Spiritual Language 35

Discovering Family Relationships 39

Discovering Family Relationships – Student Handout 41

Learning to Talk to Daddy 45

Learning to Talk to Daddy – Student Handout 47

Discovering How to Walk 51

Discovering How to Walk – Student Handout 55

Discovering How to Share the Excitement 59

Discovering How to Share the Excitement – Student Handout 63

Discovering My Family Identity and Structure 67

Discovering My Family Identity and Structure – Student Handout 69

Discovering What My Family Believes 73

Discovering How to Resolve Family Differences 75

Discovering How the Family Budget Works 79

Discovering How the Family Budget Works – Student Handout 81

Discovering the Key to The Family's Blessing 85

Discovering the Key to The Family's Blessing – Student Handout 87

Discovering the Joy of Family Commitment 91

Church Membership Application 93

Introduction

Jesus Christ was having one of His last conversations with the disciples before returning to Heaven. He had arranged this meeting with the eleven in a special mountain location of Galilee. He wanted to impress upon them, one more time, the critical importance of their future work and of the mission God was entrusting to them. When the eleven arrived at the meeting place they began worshipping the Savior, although, some still doubted His resurrection and were very much in question of their future.

"All power is given unto Me, in heaven and on earth..." – Jesus began. He continued:

"Go and make disciples of all nations, baptizing them in the Name of the Father and of the Son and of the Holy Spirit"[1]

The fulfillment of that command became the passion and the vision that has impacted the world for two millenniums and has changed the very course of history. The impact upon Jerusalem was so dramatic in the early months the leaders declared, *"Behold, you have filled Jerusalem with your doctrine"*[2]. The vision to fulfill Jesus' command continued growing over the months and years after His ascension, reaching greater and greater masses of the Roman Empire. One city declared, *"These that have turned the world upside down are come hither also"*[3]. The Great Commission was being so effectively fulfilled, that all of Asia Minor, both Jews and Greeks, heard the Gospel of Jesus Christ in just two years.

The power of the Gospel of Jesus Christ has the same impact upon cities and regions, today, when a local church, or community of churches, catches the vision and passion of the Great Commission. George Otis, Jr. has documented the modern-day impact of Jesus' command in two videos: "Transformation" and "Transformations II".

Making disciples is the most important work of the Church and it is the most effective means for transforming homes, cities and communities. It will raise up prayer warriors and intercessors. Anointed and effective workers will be equipped for the various ministries. The foundation for loyal and dedicated leaders will be established. The torch for advancing the Kingdom of God will be passed on to the next generation!

Making disciples requires much time and it is extremely labor intensive. There is no greater joy and excitement experienced in a family than when a newborn baby is brought home from the hospital. It is the same for the family of God when effective discipleship ministry is taking place. The pastor and the congregation have the privilege of watching newborn babies grow into maturity.

---

[1] Matthew 28:18-19
[2] Acts 5:28
[3] Acts 17:6

God's heart is passionate about seeing His children grow into Christ-like maturity and become effective ambassadors for His Kingdom. The pastor and local church who will make the choice to give discipleship top priority and quality effort will receive a great reward. The Heavenly Father will be glorified; Jesus Christ will be exalted and the fruit of their labor will remain. (John 15:8-16)

The Holy Spirit birthed a vision in my heart in the late 1970's. God was graciously giving new converts to our ministry and I longed to see them grow and become mighty in Spirit. The resources I found were very few. The majority of the discipleship material that was available did not teach the new believer how to receive the gift of the baptism of the Holy Spirit or how to walk in the power of an anointed life. The Spirit-filled resources on the market lacked depth and balance. I began earnestly seeking the Lord, asking Him to help me write material for the new believers He was giving to our ministry. I longed to see the new believer become mature, filled with the Holy Spirit and effective in "doing the work of the ministry". (Eph. 4:12) I also wanted to train the established believers, so they could become effective in sharing their faith, praying for others and able to train new disciples themselves.

The teaching outlines in this manual are the result of over twenty years of teaching discipleship courses and equipping young believers for Kingdom service. These teachings have literally been covered with hours of intercession and soaked with many tears. My heart has been filled with joy as I have watched those who knew little of the Scriptures or of Jesus Christ, grow to maturity and become established as strong disciples. I have rejoiced, watching established believers become effective workers who were "able to teach others also" (II Timothy 2:2). Some of those disciples are in full time Christian ministry today and others are effective missionaries in their work place. My prayer is that you will find the great joy and reward I have found in sharing these teachings.

> *"By this is My Father glorified, that you bear much fruit, and so prove to be My disciples... You did not choose Me, but I chose you, and appointed you, that you should go and bear fruit, and that your fruit should remain, that whatever you ask of the Father in My name, He may give to you. This I command you, that you love one another."*[4]

---

[4] John 15:8, 16-17 (NAS)

Experiencing New Life - Student

I. **The need in every heart**

   A. The first question we must ask ourselves is what does God require for entrance into heaven?

   1. Jesus answered that question in Matt. 5:48
   2. God requires perfection
   3. How many know someone here who is perfect?
   4. Then who is going to heaven? – No one... why?

   B. No one on earth is perfect...

   1. Romans 3:10
   2. Romans 3:23

   C. Why is everyone on earth unrighteous?
   - Psalm 51:1-5 - every human being is born with a sinful heart

   D. What is the result?
   - Romans 6:23 - the wages of sin is death

II. **The awesome solution**

   A. God loves mankind but He is a righteous and holy God and must punish sin

   B. God entered the world in the person of Jesus Christ
   - John 1:1-12
   - John 3:16
   - Jesus was a man but He was also God - all man but also all God
   - Col. 2:9, 10
   - Jesus is "Savior" - He saves you from those things which you cannot save yourself from- Matthew 1:21 "What in your life can you not save yourself from?"
   - Jesus is "Lord" - He has all authority in heaven and earth (Matt. 28:18) "If you made a table or painted a painting, how much authority over it would you have? Why?"

   C. Why did Jesus come to earth?
   - Romans 5:8-9

   While we were still sinners Jesus died for us. Through His death and the spilling of His blood we are saved from wrath.

D. How does that work?
1. Jesus was nailed to the Cross on Calvary taking our sins with Him
   - Isa. 53:5-6
   - II Cor. 5:21
   - Rom. 6:6-7
2. Jesus was buried and our sins were buried with Him
   - Rom. 6:1-3
3. Jesus rose from the dead so we could live a new life free from sin
   - Rom. 6:4, 11

III. How can a person receive a new life?

A. Believe that Jesus is who God says He is
   - Romans 10:9-10
B. Confess your sin to God and ask His forgiveness
   - I John 1:9

   "Confessing" is being willing to admit what God says about your life and sin is correct and you want to change it

C. Repent of your life of sin

   Matt. 4:17 - Jesus preached repentance everywhere He went

   Luke 13:5 - Jesus said if we do not repent we will perish

   Acts 3:19 - when we repent our sins are wiped out forever

   1. *"Repent"* means to have a change of mind about our sin - we think about it differently and see it for what it really is and it is repugnant to us.
   2. *"Repent"* means to have a change of emotion about our sin - we are sorrowful for the way we have offended God and hurt others.
   3. *"Repent"* means to have a change of direction with our life - we never want to go that way again - we choose to turn our life completely around.
   4. "Repent" - asking God to give us a new heart so we can live differently.

D. Receive Jesus Christ into your heart
   - John 1:12
     1. Ask Jesus to come live in and through you
     2. Ask Jesus Christ to become the Lord and Savior of your life

IV. What happens next?

    A. When you receive Jesus Christ you have received new life

        1. John 3:1-7 - you have been born again - received a new life

        2. II Peter 1:4 - you have received a new life source

    B. You must learn how to live out of that new life source

        1. Romans 8:1-4 - the Holy Spirit within you enables you to live a new life

        2. Gal. 5:16, 24-25 – the character qualities of Jesus Christ are shaped within your life by the Holy Spirit *(this material is covered in the study of Discipleship 101)*

Experiencing New Life – Student Handout

I. **The need in every heart**

   A. The first question we must ask ourselves is what does God require for entrance into heaven?

      1. _____

      2. _____

      3. _____

      4. _____

   B. No one on earth is perfect…

      1. Romans 3:10

      2. Romans 3:23

   C. Why is everyone on earth unrighteous?

     - Psalm 51:1-5 - _____

   D. What is the result?

     - Romans 6:23 - _____

II. **The awesome solution**

   A. God loves mankind but He is a _____ God and must punish sin

   B. God entered the world in the _____

     - John 1:1-12

     - John 3:16

- Jesus was a _____ but He was also God - all man but also all God

- Col. 2:9, 10

- Jesus is "_____" - He saves you from those things which you cannot save yourself from- Matthew 1:21 "What in your life can you not save yourself from?"

- Jesus is "_____" - He has all authority in heaven and earth (Matt. 28:18) "If you made a table or painted a painting, how much authority over it would you have? Why?"

C. Why did Jesus come to earth?

- Romans 5:8-9

_____

_____

How does that work?

1. Jesus was _____

    - Isa. 53:5-6

    - II Cor. 5:21

    - Rom. 6:6-7

2. Jesus was _____

    - Rom. 6:1-3

3. Jesus

    _____

    - Rom. 6:4, 11

III. How can a person receive a new life?

A. Believe _____

- Romans 10:9-10

B. Confess _____

- I John 1:9

"Confessing" is being willing to admit what God says about your life and sin is correct and you want to change it

C. Repent _____

Matt. 4:17 - Jesus preached repentance everywhere He went

Luke 13:5 - Jesus said if we do not repent we will perish

Acts 3:19 - when we repent our sins are wiped out forever

1. *"Repent"* means to have a _____ about our sin - we think about it differently and see it for what it really is and it is repugnant to us.

2. *"Repent"* means to have a _____ about our sin - we are sorrowful for the way we have offended God and hurt others.

3. *"Repent"* means to have a _____ with our life - we never want to go that way again - we choose to turn our life completely around.

4. "Repent" - asking God to give us a new heart so we can live _____

D. Receive Jesus Christ into your heart

- John 1:12

1. Ask Jesus to _____

2. Ask Jesus Christ _____

15

IV. What happens next?

    A. When you receive Jesus Christ you have received _____

        1. John 3:1-7 - you have been born again - received a new life

        2. II Peter 1:4 - you have received a new life _____

    B. You must learn how to live out of that new life source

        1. Romans 8:1-4 - _____

        2. Gal. 5:16, 24-25 – the character qualities of Jesus Christ are shaped within your life by the Holy Spirit *(this material is covered in the study of Discipleship 101)*

Notes

Discovering the Mark of the Family Covenant

(Scriptural teaching on water baptism)

I. **Is water baptism commanded for the believer?**

   A. It was commanded by Jesus Christ
   - Matthew 28:19
   - Mark 16:15-16

   B. It was taught by Jesus Christ's disciples
   - Acts 2:38
   - Acts 9:17-18
   - Acts 8:16
   - Acts 10:47-48
   - Acts 8:36-38
   - Acts 19:1-6

II. **What is the purpose and meaning of water baptism?**

   A. It is a declaration that we have fully identified with Jesus Christ's death, burial and resurrection and we are born again and raised to new life, Romans 6:1-7.

   B. It is a declaration that we have been baptized by the Holy Spirit into the body of Jesus Christ, I Cor. 12:13.

   C. It is our seal of the family covenant as a son and daughter of God, just as circumcision was the seal of covenant for Abraham, Col. 2:10-12.

III. When should a person be baptized in water?

   A. There are many different teachings by denominations

   1. Infant baptism gives you entrance into heaven
   2. Water baptism is a door of entrance into church membership
   3. Water baptism is the means of repentance and conversion
   4. None of the above are even taught in Scripture and they are not biblical.

   B. What is the teaching in Scripture for when a person should be baptized?

   1. Matthew 3:6-8 - John the Baptist - people confessed their sins and brought forth fruit to show they truly had repented and could be baptized in water.
   2. Mark 16:15-16 - Jesus taught the disciples to baptize those who believed and were saved.
   3. Acts 2:38 - Peter commanded the people to repent and then be baptized.
   4. Acts 8:12 - Philip baptized those who believed his preaching about the Kingdom of God and believed in Jesus Christ.

5. Acts 8:35-38 - Philip baptized the man who believed Jesus was the Son of God
6. Acts 10:44-48 - Peter baptized the people after they had believed and received the Holy Spirit
7. Acts 19:1-7 - the apostle Paul baptized the men after they had been instructed regarding Jesus Christ and believed in Him.

Each of these Scriptures teaches water baptism should follow repentance, faith in Jesus Christ and conversion.

C. When should a person be baptized...?
1. ... not before they have repented and been converted.
2. ... not in place of or to preclude repentance and conversion.
3. ... not for the purpose of bringing repentance and conversion
4. ... only after the person has repented and been saved.
5. ... if they have been a religious person and have come to true saving faith (even if they have been baptized earlier in life).
6. Matt. 3:1-11 - John the Baptist was baptizing Jews, even religious leaders
7. Acts 9:17-18 - Saul a very devote Jew came to true saving faith
8. Acts 19:1-7 - followers of John the Baptist came to salvation and were re-baptized

IV. What should be the method of water baptism?

A. The element being used is water
1. Matthew 3:11
2. Acts 8:38

B. The minister of the Gospel is the agent
1. Matthew 3:1-6
2. John 4:1-2
3. Acts 8:38-39
4. Acts 19:1-7

C. The new believer is the candidate
1. Mark 16:15-16
2. Acts 16:30-34

D. Immersion is the method
    1. The very meaning of the word baptize - "immerse a garment in dye"
    2. Acts 8:38-39 - they went down into the water
    3. The whole person is to go under the water and be lifted out again as identification with Jesus death, burial and resurrection
    4. Immersion is the only true way of carrying this out.

E. "In the name of the Father, Son and the Holy Spirit" is the formula
    1. Matthew 28:19
    2. Jesus' personal instructions were to baptize the believers in the name of the Father and of the Son and of the Holy Spirit.
    3. The person is being baptized into the family name and becoming one with the Father, Son and Holy Spirit
    4. It is like the bride taking the husband's family name and becoming one with him.

Discovering the Mark of the Family Covenant – Student Handout

(Scriptural teaching on water baptism)

I. **Is water baptism commanded for the believer?**

    A. It was commanded by _____

    B. It was taught by _____

II. **What is the purpose and meaning of water baptism?**

    A. _____

    B. _____

    C. _____

III. **When should a person be baptized in water?**

    A. _____

        1. _____

        2. _____

        3. _____

        4. _____

    B. _____

C. When should a person be baptized?

1. _____

2. _____

3. _____

4. _____

5. _____

6. _____

7. _____

8. _____

IV. **What should be the method of water baptism?**

A. _____

  1. Matthew 3:11

  2. Acts 8:38

B. _____

C. _____

D. _____

E. _____

Notes

Notes

Notes

Discovering Family Relationships

I. What is the Church?

(The following is an example of a vision and mission statement)

A. Our identity:

        Loyalty

        Integrity

        Friendship

        Teamwork

B. Our mission:

"A life-giving church where faith becomes reality"

C. Our vision:

"Win a city"

D. Our affiliation:

Living Faith Church is affiliated with the Church of God, Cleveland, TN. However, our ministry emphasis is upon the community and meeting the needs of individuals who live within our community.

II. How do I know which local church God wants me to become come a part of?

A. The church should have a biblical vision

- Matt. 16:18; Matt. 28:19; Mark 16:14-18; Acts 1:8; 2:41-43; 26:19-20

   Each of these Scriptures share the vision Jesus and the apostles had for the church

B. You must be able to agree with the leadership, philosophy and style

- Prov. 6:16-19; 1 Thess. 5:12-13; Heb. 13:17

C. There should be a place for you to help fulfill the vision

- Rom. 12:4-8; Eph. 4:16

D. You and your family must be fed spiritually

- John 24:15-17; 1 peter 5:1-4; Ez. 34:11-16

E. You must know that the Holy Spirit has placed you in that local church

- I Cor. 12:13-18

Discovering Family Relationships – Student Handout

I. **What is the Church?**

   (The following is an example of a vision and mission statement)

   A. Our identity:

   > Loyalty
   >
   > Integrity
   >
   > Friendship
   >
   > Teamwork

   B. Our mission:

   "A life-giving church where faith becomes reality"

   C. Our vision:

   "Win a city"

   D. Our affiliation:

   Living Faith Church is affiliated with the Church of God, Cleveland, TN. However, our ministry emphasis is upon the community and meeting the needs of individuals who live within our community.

II. **How do I know which local church God wants me to become come a part of?**

   A. The church should have a _____

   - Matt. 16:18; Matt. 28:19; Mark 16:14-18; Acts 1:8; 2:41-43; 26:19-20

     Each of these Scriptures share the vision Jesus and the apostles had for the church

   B. You must be able to _____ with the leadership, philosophy and style

   - Prov. 6:16-19; 1 Thess. 5:12-13; Heb. 13:17

   C. There should be a place for you to _____

- Rom. 12:4-8; Eph. 4:16

D. You and your family must be _____

- John 24:15-17; 1 peter 5:1-4; Ez. 34:11-16

E. You must know that _____
in that local church

- I Cor. 12:13-18

Notes

Learning to Talk to Daddy

I. **The call to prayer - Luke 18:1**

- The Apostles made prayer the priority of the church - Ephesians 6:18 / I Timothy 2:8
- James 5:13-17
- Jesus said that prayer should be a normal way of life - Matthew 6:9-12

II. **The joyful assurance of prayer**

A. Prayers that have been answered

- Joshua 6 (the whole chapter)
- Joshua 10:12-14
- I Kings 17 (the whole chapter) / James 5:14-16
- II Kings 19:1-36
- Acts 9:32-36
- Acts 20:1-12

B. You can have answered prayers also

- John 14:13-14
- John 15:7, 16
- James 5:14-17

III. **Some important instructions about prayer**

A. Believe God hears and answers - Mark 11:22-24

B. Keep a heart free from unforgiveness - Mark 11:25, 26 / Matthew 6:14, 15

C. Prayer is a learned skill, just as English is a learned skill - Luke 11:1

D. Use the model Jesus gave, in the beginning to assist you in prayer - as a child does with a parent - Luke 11:2-4 / Matthew 6:9-13

- Praise and worship
- God's will and intervention into life's situations
- Daily needs
- Forgive all who have offended
- Ask forgiveness for all you have offended, including your sins against God
- Grace and wisdom to avoid temptations and sins
- Put on the armor of God
- Praise and worship again

E. Be earnest and persistent in prayer - Luke 11:5-10

F. Believe your Heavenly Father wants to bless you and answer your prayers -

- Luke 11:11-13 / Matthew 7:7-11

Learning to Talk to Daddy – Student Handout

I. **The _____ to prayer - Luke 18:1**

   - The Apostles made prayer the priority of the church - Ephesians 6:18 / I Timothy 2:8

   - James 5:13-17

   - Jesus said that prayer should be a normal way of life - Matthew 6:9-12

II. **The _____ of prayer**

   A. Prayers that have been answered

   - Joshua 6 (the whole chapter)

   - Joshua 10:12-14

   - I Kings 17 (the whole chapter) / James 5:14-16

   - II Kings 19:1-36

   - Acts 9:32-36

   - Acts 20:1-12

   B. You can have answered prayers also

   - John 14:13-14

   - John 15:7, 16

   - James 5:14-17

III. **Some important _____ about prayer**

   A. Believe God hears and answers - Mark 11:22-24

   B. Keep a heart free from unforgiveness - Mark 11:25, 26 / Matthew 6:14, 15

   C. Prayer is a learned skill, just as English is a learned skill - Luke 11:1

   D. Use the model Jesus gave, in the beginning to assist you in prayer - as a child does with a parent - Luke 11:2-4 / Matthew 6:9-13

- Praise and worship
- God's will and intervention into life's situations
- Daily needs
- Forgive all who have offended
- Ask forgiveness for all you have offended, including your sins against God
- Grace and wisdom to avoid temptations and sins
- Put on the armor of God
- Praise and worship again

E. Be earnest and persistent in prayer - Luke 11:5-10

F. Believe your Heavenly Father wants to bless you and answer your prayers
  -
  - Luke 11:11-13 / Matthew 7:7-11

Notes

Discovering How to Walk

INTRODUCTION:

What it is like when you bring a new baby home from the hospital?

- little sleep

- new noises around the house (crying, etc.)

- new demands - feeding, baths, diapers, etc.

What are some things the child must learn as they grow up?

- how to sit up

- how to crawl

- how to walk

- how to talk

It is the same way in our Christian life - new changes have come - new things must be learned if we are to walk with the Lord.

Jesus said to Peter, James and John then later to Matthew "Follow Me" - that is "come walk with Me and go where I go and live like I live".

They had to learn a new way of life and so must you.

I. **Learn to eat the right food to have strength**

    A. 1 PETER 2:1-2 (NAS)

> *"Therefore, putting aside all malice and all guile and hypocrisy and envy and all slander, like newborn babes, long for the pure milk of the Word, that by It you may grow in respect to salvation,"*

        1. They needed to recognize they were adults physically but new babies spiritually

        2. They need the kind of food that would help them to grow as spiritual babes

        3. It needed to be the pure milk of the Word of God

        4. Don't try to understand the book of Revelation, or all the hard teachings of the Bible right away

        5. Take the basics and learn them (like the class we are now in and Discipleship 101)

        6. Trust God for the parts you do not understand immediately, it will come!

    B. Read the Word every day

1. Every morning read in St. John and then move to the book of Acts and Philippians
2. Pray before you read, "God this is your Word to me, please speak to me from it, this morning."
3. Read till something stands out – stop, think on what it is saying to you for a few moments and then go on reading until one more thing stands out. Stop and think on that for a time.
4. Once two things have stood out to you don't read any more that morning. Spend your day thinking on those two things God spoke to you.
5. Read Proverbs every evening - one chapter for every day of the month

C. Set aside time for special studies

1. Saturday morning or evening and Sunday afternoons are great times
2. Use your Bible concordance and look up topics like worry, fear, hope, etc.
3. Read all the verses related to those and mark them and keep notes in a binder.
4. Read about the lives of great men and women in the Bible and keep notes on who they were, where they lived, the time they lived in and events in their lives such as great deeds, personal failures and how they handled those. Make special notes about how God dealt with them and revealed Himself to them and their lives.

II. Learn the joy and the power of obedience

A. Jesus learned obedience

John 5:19-31

Hebrews 5:7-9

B. We are to learn obedience as children of God the same as Jesus

John 15:1-14

C. Steps to obedience

1. Purpose in your heart you will be obedient before you know what the Word will say to you
2. Purpose in your heart you will obey no matter what it costs you
3. Set your heart to love God with all your heart for love is the key to obedience
4. When you disobey, ask His forgiveness quickly without delaying it

D. Important points to remember about obedience

1. Obedience is a choice not a feeling - good feelings come from obedience not the other way around

2. Obedience is a training and a learning process that requires teaching, practice, discipline, doing it over and over again to establish good habits and right behavior (just like a child learning to walk, eat with manners, etc.)

3. Expect God to discipline you and even spank you when you do wrong - it is good that He loves you enough to do that (Prov. 3:11-12, Heb. 12:5-11)

4. Learn to honor and love the Lord when He allows you to go through hard places for it is the training ground of His children to learn obedience and how to walk as mature sons and daughters

III. Steps to consistently reading the Bible

A. Get a translation you can understand (NIV or NAS)

B. Set a specific time each day

C. Establish a specific place to read each day

D. Before you begin reading ask God, "this is your Word, please speak to me from it, today. I open my heart to hear your Word."

E. Read until something stands out to you, then stop, don't read any further until you have thought on that which stood out. After a few minutes continue reading until something else stands out. Stop! Don't read any more at this time. Spend the day thinking on what God spoke to from those two passages.

IV. Five questions to ask when you read the bible

A. What is God saying to me?

B. Is there a promise I am to claim?

C. Is there an example in here I am to follow?

D. Is there a sin that I am to avoid in my life?

E. Is there a command that I am to obey?

Discovering How to Walk – Student Handout

I. **Learn to eat the right food to have strength**

    A. 1 PETER 2:1-2 (NAS)

> "Therefore, putting aside all malice and all guile and hypocrisy and envy and all slander, like newborn babes, long for the pure milk of the Word, that by It you may grow in respect to salvation,"

    B. Read the Word every day

        1. _____

        2. _____

        3. _____

        4. _____

        5. _____

    C. Set aside time for special studies

II. **Learn the joy and the power of obedience**

    A. _____

        John 5:19-31

        Hebrews 5:7-9

    B. _____

        John 15:1-14

C. Steps to obedience

1. _____
2. _____
3. _____
4. _____

D. Important points to _____

1. _____
_____
2. _____
_____
3. _____
_____
4. _____
_____

III. **Steps to consistently reading the Bible**

A. Get a translation you can understand (NIV or NAS)

B. Set a specific time each day

C. Establish a specific place to read each day

D. Before you begin reading ask God, "this is your Word, please speak to me from it, today. I open my heart to hear your Word."

E. Read until something stands out to you, then stop, don't read any further until you have thought on that which stood out. After a few minutes continue reading until something else stands out. Stop! Don't read any more at this time. Spend the day thinking on what God spoke to from those two passages.

IV. **Five questions to ask when you read the bible**

    A. What is God saying to me?

    B. Is there a promise I am to claim?

    C. Is there an example in here I am to follow?

    D. Is there a sin that I am to avoid in my life?

    E. Is there a command that I am to obey?

Notes

Discovering How to Share the Excitement

I. **The call to share your faith**

- Mark 8:34-38

    Jesus defines a disciple as someone who has surrendered his life completely. A disciple also is someone who loves Jesus Christ with all his being and is not ashamed of Him no matter how unpopular or intimidating the crowd or the circumstances around them. Wherever we are and whatever we are doing we must be a light, a witness!

- I Peter 3:15-16

    Peter exhorts the disciples to always be ready to give a reason for the hope that is now in your heart. Because you have received Jesus you have a hope you did not have before and a hope the people around you do not have. You must be ready to give a reason for that hope that is within you. That is what this lesson is about.

- I Peter 4:10

    Peter said, we are all stewards of God's grace. Steward is someone who is a manager of someone's property. We are stewards of God's grace. That means if grace is going into your work place, it comes through you. If grace is going to reach your family, neighborhood, friends, it is through you. Are you prepared to be a steward of God's grace?

CATCH A VISION

The world around, the people around you, family, friends, neighbors, coworkers are as lost or even more lost than you were. They are going to hell, no question! They will be lost eternally with no hope. You have the answer. You have the life jacket to save them. Will you remain silent, indifferent, unmoved by their condition?

When you can help, will you do nothing?

II. **The tools to share your testimony**

This is the greatest tool you have for sharing your hope and faith. You are never at the mercy of an argument when you have a testimony. Your testimony is telling someone what you have seen, heard and experienced. All of you can do that. We will have opportunity in a moment to develop that.

1. Some guidelines

    - In a few moments we're going to learn a simple outline for sharing your faith. Keep it simple so people can understand.

    - Keep it kind and gracious so people can receive it.

    - Keep it hopeful and exciting so people want it.

    - Get permission so people are open to it. "May I tell you what happened to me?"

2. Divine appointments
   - Pray daily for divine appointments to share.
   - Look for those opportunities God sends you way.
   - Scatter seeds at each opportunity, only if it is just a word or two.
   - Make a prayer list of your family, coworkers, neighbors, enemies and pray daily

III.   A simple outline

1. Grace
- No one deserves or can earn God's gift of eternal life.
- It is an absolute free gift.
- Most people are trying to earn their way – "treat my neighbor right, not too bad, keep the Ten Commandments". Why it cannot be earned is understood when we know what God says about man.

2. Man
   - Mankind is a sinner - hopelessly, helplessly, habitually a sinner.
   - He is born that way and cannot change himself.
   - God requires perfection (Matt. 5:48) to get to heaven, no one is going to heaven.
   - We understand that better when we understand what the Bible says about God.

3. God
   - God is perfect and just. He hates sin and must properly punish sinners.
   - God is also love - He loves you and me and does not want to punish us for the sin.
   - God has a dilemma, how can He get us to heaven when we must be perfect, but we are sinners and he must punish sin. Yet He loves us desperately. He solved this dilemma in an amazing way...

4. Christ
   - God entered the world in the person of Jesus Christ.
   - Jesus was man but He was also ALL GOD
   - He took our place and He took our sins upon Himself. He paid the penalty for the sins we have committed. But, He also rose from the dead on the third day.
   - He died so we would not have to die. He rose from the dead so we could have eternal life.
   - The way to experience this wonder provision is by faith...

5. Faith
    - Faith is not mere intellectual ascent.
    - Faith is not a "fox-hole conversion." - crying out to God when you I am in trouble and then forgetting about it after the crisis is over.
    - Faith is placing my absolute trust in Him alone for what He has done for me.
    - I open my heart and ask Him to forgive me of my sin and to come live in my life.

Do you understand this? Is there any reason you could not receive Jesus Christ right now?

Discovering How to Share the Excitement – Student Handout

I. **The call to share your faith**

- Mark 8:34-38

- I Peter 3:15-16

- I Peter 4:10

CATCH A VISION

The world around, the people around you, family, friends, neighbors, coworkers are as lost or more lost than you were. They are going to hell, no question! They will be lost eternally with no hope. You have the answer. You have the life jacket to save them. Will you remain silent, indifferent, unmoved by their condition?

When you can help, will you do nothing?

II. **The tools to share your testimony**

Your _____
_____
_____

1. Some _____

    - Keep it _____ so people can receive it.

    - Keep it _____ so people want it.

    - Get _____ so people are open to it. "May I tell you what happened to me?"

2. Divine _____

    - _____ for divine appointments to share.

    - Look for those _____ God sends you way.

- _____ at each opportunity, only if it is just a word or two.

- Make a _____ of your family, coworkers, neighbors, enemies and pray daily

III. A simple outline

1. _____

2. _____

3. _____

4. _____

5. _____

Notes

Discovering My Family Identity and Structure

I. **What did the Church look like in the New Testament?**

   A. The church is people - I Cor. 1:1-3

   1. Called by the Holy Spirit

   2. Sanctified - made holy by God's forgiveness

   3. "In Christ" - Christ "in" them by the Holy Spirit

   B. The church is covenant people (family) – I Cor. 1:9

   1. "Koinonia" - "fellowship" - relationship by covenant

   2. … with the Father and with the Son

   3. … with one another

   C. The church is people who live by a different motivation than the world – they live by the Holy Spirit – I Cor. 2:4, 9-10

   1. Spirit empowered

   2. Spirit motivated

   3. Spirit directed

   4. Spirit disciplined

   D. The church is - people led by a servant leader who is not seeking a following for himself

   1. They are stewards of God's house - not their ownership

   2. They understand Jesus builds the church - we sows and water - God gives the increase

   3. They lead as a father leads his family

II. **The role of each member of the leadership team**

   1. Senior pastor - vision, oversight, main teacher, C.E.O.

   2. Elder board - staff pastors who team up with the senior pastor, lead various ministries, board of directors for the local ministry, trains workers

   3. Deacon and deaconess - care givers, serve in the various ministries, advisers to pastoral staff, assist in leadership

III. **The five leadership paradigms**

   A. The Domination Model – King Saul – I Samuel 14:20-30

   1. Self-centered

   2. Controlling

   3. Non-relational

   4. Harsh – does not think of his people and who makes him successful

B. The Isolation Model – King Uzziah – I Chronicles 26:1-23
   1. Results centered
   2. Non-affirming
   3. Non-relational
   4. Harsh – does not think of his people and who makes him successful

C. The Administration Model – King Solomon – I Kings 4:1-34
   1. Task oriented
   2. Reward based affirmation
   3. Minimal relationship
   4. Less harsh but tend to use people to reach a goal

D. The Coaching Model – Apostle Paul – II Timothy 1:1-7
   1. Person centered
   2. Affirming with rewards, praise, touch
   3. Highly relational
   4. Seeks to build the individual because his success is seen through those who are around him

E. The Servant Leader Model – Jesus – John 13:1-17
   1. Person centered
   2. Affirming with rewards, praise, touch
   3. Highly relational
   4. Seeks to meet individual needs with care and compassion and lays his life down for the people he leads

IV. **Accountability**

A. Accountability is critical to effective ministry
B. The senior pastor is accountable to the church elder board
C. The staff pastors are accountable to the senior pastor and the elder board.
D. The leadership team is accountable in areas of integrity, moral purity, and financial integrity, handling the congregation in love and grace, family life, doctrinal truth.

Discovering My Family Identity and Structure – Student Handout

I. **What did the Church look like in the New Testament?**

    A. _____ - I Cor. 1:1-3

    B. The church is _____ - I Cor. 1:9

        "Koinonia" _____

    C. The church is people who live by a different motivation that the world –

    _____

    _____

    I Cor. 2:4, 9-10

    D. The church is - people led by a servant leader who is not seeking a following for himself

    I Cor. 3:5-10; 4:1-2

II. **The role of each member of the leadership team**

1. Senior pastor - vision, oversight, main teacher, C.E.O.
2. Elder board - staff pastors who team up with the senior pastor, lead various ministries, board of directors for the local ministry, trains workers
3. Deacon and deaconess - care givers, serve in the various ministries, advisers to pastoral staff, assist in leadership

III. **The five leadership paradigms**

    A. _____

    I Samuel 14:20-30

        1. _____

       2. _____

       3. _____

       4. _____

   B. _____

   I Chronicles 26:1-23

       1. _____

       2. _____

       3. _____

       4. _____

   C. _____

   I Kings 4:1-34

       1. _____

       2. _____

       3. _____

       4. _____

   D. _____

   II Timothy 1:1-7

       1. _____

       2. _____

       3. _____

       4. _____

   E. _____

   John 13:1-17

       1. _____

       2. _____

       3. _____

       4. _____

IV.   **Accountability**

Notes

Discovering What My Family Believes

STATEMENT OF FAITH

We Believe…

1. … In the verbal inspiration of the Bible.
2. … In one God eternally existing in three persons; namely the Father, Son and Holy Ghost.
3. … That Jesus Christ is the only begotten Son of the Father, conceived of the Holy Ghost, and born of the Virgin Mary; that Jesus was crucified, buried and raised from the dead; that He ascended to heaven and is today at the right hand of the Father as the Intercessor.
4. … That all have sinned and come short of the glory of God and that repentance is commanded of God for all and necessary for the forgiveness of sins.
5. … That justification, regeneration, and the new birth are wrought by faith in the blood of Jesus Christ.
6. … In sanctification through identification with the death, burial and resurrection of Jesus Christ and by the power of the Holy Spirit.
7. … Holiness to be God's standard of living for His people.
8. … In the baptism with the Holy Spirit subsequent to a clean heart.
9. … In speaking with other tongues as the Spirit gives utterance and that it is the initial evidence of the baptism in the Holy Ghost.
10. … In water baptism by immersion and that all who repent should be baptized in the name of the Father and of the Son, and of the Holy Spirit
11. … Divine healing is provided for all in the atonement.
12. … In the Lord's Supper and washing of the saints' feet.
13. … In the pre-millennial second coming of Jesus - first to resurrect the righteous dead and to catch away the living saints to Him in the air, second, to reign on the earth a thousand years.
14. … In the bodily resurrection; eternal life for the righteous and eternal punishment for the wicked.

We also believe…

1. … The leadership gifts, Apostle, Prophet, Evangelist, Pastor, Teacher, given by Jesus Christ when He rose from the dead, are for the church today.
2. … The manifestation gifts of the Holy Spirit, word of wisdom, word of knowledge, faith, gifts of healing, working of miracles, prophecy, discerning of spirits, tongues and interpretation of tongues, are for the church today and should be expressed by individuals anointed by the Holy Spirit, who are known by the church leadership, and released for such ministry.

Notes

Discovering How to Resolve Family Differences

CHURCH POLICY OF GRIEVANCE AND ACCUSATION

I. **Statement of Intent:**

There are specified steps of reconciliation and discipline to restore a minister or a member who has been offensive, broken fellowship with the body of Christ, or participated in conduct that compromises holy living or the Christian faith. These steps of restoration are based upon biblical principles and the command to *"bear one another's burden"* and fulfill the law of Christ.

> *Brothers, if someone is caught in a sin, you who are spiritual should restore him gently. But watch yourself, or you also may be tempted. Carry each other's burdens, and in this way you will fulfill the law of Christ. (Gal. 6:1-2)*

It is the heart and the concern of the pastoral staff and the congregation to see every person who has fallen be restored spiritually and emotionally. It is our aim for them to grow into the maturity and fullness of Jesus Christ and to see them ministering in the anointing of the Holy Spirit.

II. **The Scripture Basis for This Policy:**

This policy is based upon the instructions of Jesus in Matthew 18:15-18. According to these principles the following steps will be taken to reach the stated objectives:

A. Resolving A Grievance Against A Member Or A Leader:

When a member or a leader has a grievance against the Senior Pastor, an associate pastor, a deacon, or another member of the church, he or she will be asked to take the following steps.

1. First go to that individual alone and seek harmony and reconciliation.
2. If the issue remains unresolved then ask the Senior Pastor or his appointed Associate Pastor or Deacon to go with them and meet the individual for the purpose of reconciliation.
3. If the issue continues to remain unresolved a hearing before the Board of Elders and Deacons maybe requested. If the issue is found to be valid, the offending member will be placed under accountability for resolving the issue and adjusting their behavior and relationships within the church.
4. If the issue is still unresolved further steps of discipline will be administered by the Board of Elders and Deacons including the possible removal from any position of leadership.

5. If the member refuses to accept the discipline and does not resolve the matter, steps will be taken to bring charges for possible removal of their membership.

B. Reconciliation And Discipline Of A Member:

When a member who is not pastoral staff or a deacon is involved in conduct that is not in harmony with Scripture or is morally impure, as determined by the teachings of the church, it is sufficient grounds for discipline. The policies of "Reconciliation and Accusation" will be applied in accordance with Matthew 18:15-18, Romans 16:17-18; 1 Corinthians 5:1-11; Galatians 1:8-9 and Titus 3:10-11. The following steps will be taken:

1. Upon hearing the accusation, the Senior Pastor or an Associate Pastor or Deacon appointed by him, shall investigate the report as to its validity. The investigation shall include, but not be limited to, tracing any reports back to their original source for accuracy and documentation, and identifying any evidence for validity and accuracy.

2. If the investigation shows the accusation has validity, the Senior Pastor or his appointed representative, shall go to the individual alone, and "speaking the truth in love" (Eph. 4:15) encourage them toward repentance and reconciliation with God and the church. If it is deemed important and necessary the accuser may accompany the Pastor in this visit.

3. If the member persists in the error or if they refuse repentance and reconciliation, the Senior Pastor and his appointed representative, along with one or two Deacons, shall go to the individual and again, in love, urge them to seek repentance and reconciliation. (II Thess. 3:15)

4. If the erring member will still not reconcile, the situation will be shared anonymously with the congregation for prayer and fasting. After a specified number of days, the Senior Pastor and his appointed representative, along with one or two Deacons shall again go to the individual and exhort them with loving correction.

5. If the member still persists in their error, they will be notified of a hearing before the Board of Elders and Deacons. The notice will be sent to their previously known address not less than three days prior to the hearing. They have the right to be heard and to offer testimony.

6. After the hearing with the Board of Elders and Deacons, if there is no reconciliation, the individual will be dis-fellowshipped with a public statement being read by the Senior Pastor to the congregation. The congregation will be urged to continual prayer and intercession for the individual, that through this discipline they might repent and be restored to fellowship. (1 Cor. 5:1-11)

7. Upon the confession and true repentance of a member in error, by the loving judgment of the Senior Pastor and the Board of Elders and Deacons, reconciliation and full restoration of membership will graciously be given. (Gal. 6:1-2; 2 Cor. 2:5-11)

C. Reconciliation And Discipline Of The Pastoral Staff And Deacons:

1. Steps one (1) through nine (7) of "Reconciliation and Discipline of a Member" will be followed, with the following exceptions.

    - Any accusation against a pastoral staff member must be in keeping with I Timothy 5:19-20.
    - The accusation must have two or three witnesses.
    - Pastoral staff will be disciplined before the entire congregation.
    - An accusation that is not frivolous (by judgment of the Board of Elders and Deacons), and appears to have validity, will require the pastor or deacon to be removed from their position while the investigation and the steps of "Reconciliation and Discipline of the Pastoral Staff and Deacons" are being taken.

Notes

Discovering How the Family Budget Works

Read carefully in class these two Scriptures

II Corinthians 9:1-15

I Corinthians 9:1-14

I. **Every family has a family budget**
   A. We all operate by a budget
   - Some don't know it and operate by spending whatever they have at that moment
   - Some operate by a bill to bill basis - spending all that comes in
   - Some operate on an "after the bills are paid" kind of budget
   - Some operate on a very meticulous budget and even save a little
   - But all operate on a budget

   B. God urges using a wise family budget
   - Proverbs 27:23
     - keep good inventory
     - know how much you have on hand
   - Proverbs 6:1-11
     - avoid debt
     - be like the ant that collects at the right time and saves up
     - avoid lazy habits

II. **Operating on an annual budget**
   A. How does the church receive financial resources?
      1. Like a family the church has expenses of housing, utilities, operating costs, and staff salaries
      2. There are two primary ways we receive the necessary funds to pay for these, faithful tithing and offerings of those who attend.
      3. Tithing is primarily the way we support the Pastoral Staff.
      4. Offerings are the primary way we cover additional expenses of operating the ministry.
      5. Special offerings are received for world missions, guest speakers, helping hands and other ministry opportunities that may arise.

III. **Handling finances with integrity is very important to the senior pastor and elders**

   Our Pledge:
   1. We pledge to never use pressure tactics, gimmicks or to beg for money when receiving the tithe and offerings.
   2. We pledge to teach the biblical basis for financial blessings and to pray regularly for those who need jobs and who are on fixed incomes.
   3. We pledge to teach the balanced and biblical basis for tithe and offerings
   4. We pledge to use integrity in the way the finances are received, counted, deposited and spent; and to be accountable to the congregation for the manner in which financial integrity is fulfilled.

IV. **How are these pledges fulfilled?**
   1. Offerings are received publicly by appointed ushers. Gifts, offerings, donations that are given to pastoral staff privately are appropriately given to the bookkeeper for proper accounting.
   2. Offerings are counted immediately by the bookkeeper and duly appointed counters, who use established count procedures. Pastoral staff is not allowed to be counters.
   3. Offerings are deposited immediately by the bookkeeper and proper records of the count forms and the deposit slips are maintained.
   4. Weekly financial reports and budget reviews are given to the Senior Pastor.
   5. Monthly financial reports and budget reviews are given to the Board of Elders.
   6. Quarterly financial reports are made available to the congregation and an annual financial report is given to the congregation.
   7. Annual budgets are prepared by the Board of Elders and submitted for concurrence by the congregation.
   8. Pastoral salaries are established by the Board of Elders and limits on expenditures that can be made without approval of the Board Elders and the congregation are established.
   9. Annual financial audits are conducted by certified public accountants and a report is given to the Board of Elders and the congregation.

Discovering How the Family Budget Works – Student Handout

II Corinthians 9:1-15

I Corinthians 9:1-14

I. **Every family has a family budget**

   A. We all operate by a budget

   B. God urges using a wise family budget

   - Proverbs 27:23

   - Proverbs 6:1-11

II. **Operating on an annual budget**

   A. How does the church receive financial resources?

   _____
   _____
   _____
   _____
   _____
   _____
   _____
   _____

III. **Handling finances with integrity is very important to the senior pastor and elders**

   Our Pledge:

   1. We pledge to never use pressure tactics, gimmicks or to beg for money when receiving the tithe and offerings.

   2. We pledge to teach the biblical basis for financial blessings and to pray regularly for those who need jobs and who are on fixed incomes.

3. We pledge to teach the balanced and biblical basis for tithe and offerings

4. We pledge to use integrity in the way the finances are received, counted, deposited and spent; and to be accountable to the congregation for the manner in which financial integrity is fulfilled.

IV. How are these pledges fulfilled?

_____

_____

_____

_____

_____

_____

_____

_____

_____

_____

Notes

Discovering the Key to The Family's Blessing

Read this passage very carefully

Joshua 7:1-13

What happened here?

Why did God allow the enemies of His people to defeat them after such a great victory at Jericho? Someone had touched the "devoted" thing (NIV translation)

I. **What is the "devoted" thing**

    A. Definition of the word in Hebrew

        "laqach" - 2764 Strong's Concordance - something devoted, under a ban, something devoted to God (sanctified). This word was used several times in Leviticus and Numbers for items of the wilderness tabernacle and offerings that are "devoted" to God.

        Joshua 6:15-19 - the whole city of Jericho was "devoted" to God no one was to touch anything of the spoil of that city. All the stuff was to go to God's treasury. Why?

    B. Jericho was the tithe city

        Jericho was the first victory, the first spoil of the new land as such, it was the first fruits. The tithe and all of the income that would be received from that victory belong to God - His treasury

II. **The principle of the tithe**

    A. What is a tithe?

      - It is a tenth of your gross income that God says belongs to Him alone - Malachi 3:10

    B. Established before the law of Moses and the Ten Commandments and after

      - Gen. 14:17-24 - Abraham paid tithe to Melchizedek, priest of the most high God
      - Gen. 28:16-22 - Jacob pledged to pay tithe to God
      - Joshua 6:17-19 - Jericho the tithe city
      - Prov. 3:9-10 - honor God with the first fruits - Malachi 3:8-10

    C. Jesus validated paying tithe

      - Matt. 23:23 - Jesus urged them to do the weightier things of the law and do not stop paying tithe

    D. The principles remain the same in the Old and New Testament

        1. There is a curse for not honoring the Lord's tithe

            a. The tithe is the Lord's alone - man is not to use it for himself - it is holy

  b. When a person spends the Lord's tithe on personal needs they are robbing God's treasury

  c. The tithe is to be brought into the Lord' treasury at the house where you worship

  d. When a person does not follow this principle they come under a curse:

   - cannot stand before their enemies when in battle
   - the windows of heaven are shut up
   - little things eat away their money
   - their work is not as productive

 2. There are specific promised blessings for obeying the tithe principle

  a. God fights the battles against the enemy and drives them back

  b. The Lord promised bounty in the career and increase of productivity

  c. The windows of heaven are opened to pour out blessing that cannot be contained

  d. The things that steal and destroy your income are rebuked and driven away

III. Obeying the tithe principle is the key to significant family blessings

A. Notice in Joshua the solidarity effect

- All Israel was cursed for one person disobeying
- All Israel was blessed when the issue was settled
- Your family will be the same
- The church is the same

God wants to bless your home, your business and your church. Your obedience in tithe will open the window of heaven to you, your family and church.

Discovering the Key to The Family's Blessing – Student Handout

Joshua 7:1-13

I. **What is the "devoted" thing**

    C. Definition of the word in Hebrew

        "*Laqach*" - 2764 Strong's Concordance - something devoted, under a ban, something devoted to God (sanctified). This word was used several times in Leviticus and Numbers for items of the wilderness tabernacle and offerings that are "devoted" to God.

    Joshua 6:15-19

    D. Jericho was _____

II. **The principle of the tithe**

    A. What is a tithe?

      - It is a tenth of your gross income that God says belongs to Him alone - Malachi 3:10

    B. Established before the law of Moses and Ten Commandments and after

      - Gen. 14:17-24 - Abraham paid tithe to Melchizedek, priest of the most high God

      - Gen. 28:16-22 - Jacob pledged to pay tithe to God

      - Joshua 6:17-19 - Jericho the tithe city

      - Prov. 3:9-10 - honor God with the first fruits - Malachi 3:8-10

    C. Jesus validated paying tithe

- Matt. 23:23 - Jesus urged them to do the weightier things of the law and do not stop paying tithe

D. The principles remain the same in the Old and New Testament

1. _____
_____
_____
_____
_____
_____
_____

2. _____
_____
_____
_____
_____

III. **Obeying the tithe principle is the key to significant family blessings**

B. Notice in Joshua the solidarity effect

_____
_____
_____
_____
_____

God wants to bless your home, your business and your church. Your obedience in tithe will open the window of heaven to you, your family and church.

Notes

Discovering the Joy of Family Commitment

Read

Acts 2:41-44

I Corinthians 1:1-10

Hebrews 10:23-25

God wants his children united together in a church fellowship

The believers on the day of Pentecost united with the 120 that had been together

- they attended steadfastly in fellowship,
- receiving teaching and uniting in prayer;
- They had personal times of being together.

Apostle Paul wrote to the church of Corinth:

- they were called into fellowship
- they were to be of the same mind and heart
- they were to be perfectly joined together

The Hebrews were urged to

- consider one another
- encourage one another
- exhort one another
- not to stop attending church

Why is church membership important?

... It is a covenant relationship in Christ (I Cor. 1:9)

... It is a commitment to love, encourage, strengthen and support one another

... It is a source of encouragement and support in time of need and testing

Notes

Church Membership Application

Note: The following information will be held in strict confidence and is for the purpose of ministering to you in the best way possible.

_____

Name (First M. Last)   Date of Birth

_____   _____

Street Address   City, State, ZIP

_____   _____   _____

Home Phone   Cell Phone   E-mail

_____

Place of Birth

	Y	N
1. I testify that I have been born again in accordance with the scriptural experience of John 3 and Romans 10:9-10	☐	☐
2. Have you been baptized in water by immersion? If yes, explain when and where. When: _____ Where: _____	☐	☐
3. Have you been baptized in the Holy Spirit with the evidence of speaking in tongues? **Please Note:** This is not a prerequisite for membership	☐	☐
4. I have read and am in agreement with the "Statement of Faith" of the church.	☐	☐
5. Do you presently hold membership with another local church? Name of the church: _____ Pastor _____	☐	☐
6. Are you under any disciplinary acting in the church? If yes, please describe: _____	☐	☐
7. I have read and agree with the vision and mission statement of the church.	☐	☐
8. I am willing to become an active part of the ministry of the local church. If yes, which area of ministry? _____ May I have more information about the following area(s) of ministry? _____	☐	☐
9. I have read, understand and agree to abide by the Policy of Grievance and Reconciliation of the church.	☐	☐
10. I purpose to support the ministry of the church financially through tithes and offerings as God enables me to do so.	☐	☐
11. I purpose to support the ministry of the church with my time, talents and prayers.	☐	☐

I pledge to be a member and to submit to the leadership of the church.

Signature: _____

Date: _____

OFFICIAL USE ONLY:

Date Received Into Membership: _____
Officiating Pastor: _____

Made in the USA
Middletown, DE
13 May 2017